SERMONETTES AT A LAY COMMUNION SERVICE

by

Gerald Anderson M.D. F.R.C.P

Grosvenor House
Publishing Limited

The right of Gerald Anderson to be identified as the author of this
work has been asserted in accordance with Section 78
of the Copyright, Designs and Patents Act 1988

The book cover picture is copyright to Gerald Anderson

This book is published by
Grosvenor House Publishing Ltd
Link House
140 The Broadway, Tolworth, Surrey, KT6 7HT.
www.grosvenorhousepublishing.co.uk

A CIP record for this book
is available from the British Library

ISBN 978-1-78623-838-2

By the Same Author:

Paramalignant Syndromes in Lung Cancer
Lifeline (under Gerald Ratcliffe)
Memories of an Exciting Life

To Rosemary, my lovely family
and my grandson Liam for inspired typing.

Contents

Foreword

Our church of St Michael's in Newport is now almost 130 years old. It was founded by Irish (economic) immigrants. They gave their labour free and the cost was £4000. The area was a marsh alongside the River Usk and was built on five metres of ship's ballast.

In 2006 the Rosminian Order found they had insufficient priests to serve our parish and were replaced by Diocesan clergy. In 2007 there was a profound reorganisation of the churches in West Newport and six churches were made into an All Saints Parish served by four priests, now reduced to two.

In addition to the churches the priests also supported three large hospitals and many nursing homes. The work burden on the priests was extreme and clearly drastic changes were required.

During the weekend we had previously had two masses with a daily weekday mass. These arrangements were replaced only by a single Sunday mass.

The situation seemed to bring the congregation to life. During the week we now have two lay-led services of Adoration, once a week prayer of the church and a lay-led communion service once weekly. In addition, there is a children's service during Sunday mass and a superb children's choir each with about twenty children. There are usually ten altar servers and sometimes more.

1

Previously parish priests had postponed church repair as it was too expensive and postponed them for their successors. In the last six years the congregation of this poor parish have raised £80,000 and embarked on an extensive programme of fabric repairs. The congregation has increased by about twenty percent.

I was asked to take the lay communion service and with considerable trepidation I started to give homilies. This book contains some of them.

On Unanswered Prayer

I first went out for a date with my wife Rosemary on my nineteenth birthday when we were both medical students. Within two weeks I made a firm decision that this was the woman I would marry. I existed on a moderate local authority grant topped up by my parents who were certainly not wealthy. Rosemary lived at home with her parents so her grant was very small. There was no way we would marry without abandoning our careers.

Since we first met we have always gone to mass together on Sundays. When we moved to Newport Rosemary was an active volunteer for CAFOD and the Justice and Peace movement, yet she was neither a Catholic nor baptised. People in the congregation always assumed she was a Catholic and occasionally the bolder ones would ask me why she did not go to communion. I always replied that it was because she was in a state of grave sin. It was always interesting to see the shock on their faces sometimes closely followed by a prurient desire to ask the nature of the sin but without the courage to do so. I did always subsequently explain that she was not a Catholic.

Four years ago I went to an Adoration service feeling disheartened. I prayed, as I had done every day since the age of nineteen, and asked God to make Rosemary a

Catholic. I grumbled that he had not listened and had done nothing about it.

'What have you got to say to me?' I demanded. I then realised his answer was,

'Gerald why do you not trust me?' I was overcome with remorse and prayed,

'Lord forgive me, I do trust you and leave it in Your hands.'

Ten weeks later Rosemary was baptised and received into the church.

The message:

We demand instant answers to our prayers. God's time scale is different to our own. We have to trust in him even when the response takes more than fifty years in my case.

The Asylum Seekers

One of my grandchildren was a student at Bristol University. She telephoned me to say that she was upset with the government and the press' treatment of asylum seekers, and that she intended to organise a protest march from Bristol to Cardiff over four days. It would, I was told, consist of asylum seekers and student supporters. She asked me if I would put up and feed about thirty people on a Saturday night on the last evening of the march. Being a typical doting grandfather I said this would be no problem and our parish priest kindly allowed us to use the church hall.

When they arrived I welcomed them on behalf of the parish and told them the church had been built by Irish people between 1845 – 1850 who were fleeing the Irish potato famine. In Newport they were extremely unpopular and were feared because it was believed that they carried infectious diseases and stole the jobs of the Welsh people. The asylum seekers certainly seemed to recognise this situation! The church was built at a cost of only £4000 as the people gave their work on the building for no money and collected donations from what little they had. Many a heavy drinker gave it up to donate the money to the building fund.

They asked to see inside the church and were very impressed by the priceless stained glass windows. I drew their attention to a window depicting the Holy Family fleeing into Egypt to escape the persecution of King Herod. Pointing to it I said, 'there are your asylum seekers'.

I fed them on thirty gigantic pizzas. We worried that after sleeping on the floor and feeding themselves that the hall would be a terrible mess. It was cleaner than before they had arrived.

The messages:

Like all older people I am prone to pontificate on the failings of the younger generation. Here we have a group of students marching fifteen miles a day for four days in incredible discomfort. Some of our young people are more idealistic than I was at that age.

When people are unpleasant about asylum seekers remember that the Holy Family were themselves fleeing persecution. You may feel that I seem to be very sympathetic towards asylum seekers. My wife was one. She fled India from the invading Japanese as a child and was accepted for refuge in Britain.

On Christ Curing Ten Lepers

This parable has a personal resonance for me. Thirty years ago I gave a lecture at a medical symposium in Barcelona. I reported results of treating mild pneumonia in general practice. Patients were randomised to receive either the new drug clarithromycin or the standard older drug. Both were equally effective but one quarter of the patients on the older drug had to stop taking it because of side effects, clarithromycin was evidently an advance. There was a period of questions after the presentation. A delegate pointed out that only 65% of patients attended for a follow up chest x-ray to confirm the cure. My first response was that while this was correct, it merely reflected that patients who now felt well were disinclined to attend for future tests. It sounded rather limp, then inspiration struck. I pointed out that Christ cured ten lepers but only one attended for a follow up. If the son of God could only get a 10% follow up and I had achieved 65% then I had done well. In the laughter which followed I managed to pass onto the next question.

The meaning of the parable is straightforward – we often do not thank God for the many good things which he gives us. However, like many parables there is a hidden meaning. The leper who returned was a Samaritan who were a group of people despised by the

Jews. There are several references to the Samaritans in the Gospels and they form a coherent story.

Who were these Samaritans? They still exist and in 2015 there were 777 of them in Israel. In the 722 C.E the Assyrian King Sargon conquered Israel and recorded that he moved 27,290 Jews to Babylon where they remained for 184 years until Cyrus the Great allowed them to return to Israel. The Samaritans believe that they were Jews left behind in Israel after 722 and that they are still the true Jews, and that when the Jews were moved to Babylon the Jewish belief became distorted. The major doctrinal differences are that Samaritans believe that their holy place is not Jerusalem but Mount Gerizim where they believe Isaac offered to sacrifice his son to God. In addition, they do not accept some of the books of the Old Testament. These may seem minor differences but the two faiths have a powerful dislike of each other. Jews did not associate with Samaritans. Each group believed it was wrong to contact the other, to speak to each other or to enter the other's territory.

Luke tells us how Christ sent two Apostles ahead of him to arrange accommodation in a Samaritan village. This was not in accordance with Jewish practice and shows Jesus reaching out to these despised people. In fact, the Samaritans refused to accept him because they felt anyone going on pilgrimage to Jerusalem was rejecting the law of Moses.

Luke again tells us in the story of the Good Samaritan how the Levite priest failed to help the man attacked by robbers but it was the Samaritan who rescued him. Here is a Samaritan behaving better than a Jewish priest.

John describes how Jesus asked a Samaritan woman for a drink from a well. The woman was shocked. 'You, a Jew, ask me, a Samaritan, for a drink'. For Jews, says the Gospel, do not associate with Samaritans. Jesus told her that she was living with a man who was not her husband. She was amazed and He told her he was the Christ.

The message:

We often thank God for the good things he gives us and the reference in the Gospels to the Samaritans tells us that Christ had come to save the whole world and not just the Jews.

On St Paul's
Embarrassing Epistles

St Paul was a remarkable man. Because of his beliefs he was mocked, jailed, shipwrecked and eventually crucified yet his faith never wavered.

However, in the twenty first century some of his epistles make me uneasy. This is most marked in his attitude to women which, to me, seems almost misogynistic. To give a few examples, in Corinthians I he advises that a woman who will not wear a veil should have her hair cut off and that women should remain silent at meetings. In Ephesians he advises that women should submit to their husbands in everything and in Colossians he says, 'they should give way to their husbands in everything as you should the Lord.' In the letter to Timothy he tells women not to wear expensive clothes, gold or jewellery and not to braid their hair. What a kill joy. Whenever these readings happen, with some tongue in cheek, I always say to some fairly feminist woman in the congregation 'some very sound teaching in today's epistle'. As it says on firework wrappings – light the blue touch paper and retire!

Aside from his comments of women there are two other passages that jar. In Ephesians he advises slaves to be obedient to their masters and in Thessalonians, in what I call St Paul's epistle to the Conservative Party

Conference, he commands 'do not give food to anyone who does not work.'

When we read these epistles there is a temptation to think we are much more sophisticated and our reasoning is better than that of Paul. This is so, but not because of our blinding wisdom but based on generations of thinking of others because wisdom is cumulative.

It would have seemed self-evident to Paul that women were inferior intellectually to men and remember that feminism is an invention of the last sixty years. When I was a child all women during church services wore a hat or a scarf and not to do so met with disapproval. As recently as Victorian times when a woman married, her money and chattels automatically went to her husband.

As for slavery, Paul returned the runaway Christian slave Onesimus to his master Philemon advising his to treat him not as a slave but as a brother. Again slaves were welcomed to become Christians, a rather revolutionary thing to do in those times.

A rather remarkable fact is that nowhere in the Gospels do we find Christ condemning slavery. The institution is so evil that surely he would have preached against it. I wonder if the explanation is this: Christ did speak against slavery but his teaching never emerged into the Gospels. For the Jews slavery was well recorded in the Old Testament and not condemned save when they were slaves themselves in Egypt. If the Gospels had demanded the abolition of slavery people would have thought that Christians were clearly mad. For the Romans during the first century AD probably about one third of the inhabitants of the Roman Empire were slaves. The Romans would feel any attempt to change this would cause profound economic upheaval and could destabilise the Empire. Anyone who advocated it would almost certainly be crucified.

The message:

Paul was a good man who gave his life for the Faith. He was a man of his time and it would be wrong to judge his teaching by modern criteria.

On Events Which
Influenced Beliefs

Our life experiences are all very different but for each of us there have been happenings which have had profound effects on our beliefs. For myself I can think of three.

At the age of seven my father seemed almost perfect, all knowing – anything he believed had to be true.

In 1943 the American Army came to Britain on their way to the Normandy landings in 1944. In his capacity as a captain in the Home Guard dad became friendly with the white colonel of a black American regiment. This man told him that his soldiers behaved liked animals and were not to be trusted. My father told me this which I accepted.

Behind our house was a brickyard where I would play with my friends. One day a party of black soldiers came in a lorry which they loaded with bricks by a man on the ground throwing them up to a man in the lorry. I was playing on the other side when a misaimed brick flew over the lorry and hit me on the head causing profuse bleeding. The soldiers were devastated and all hugged me and produced large amounts of chocolate – a great rarity in wartime. They treated me as though the accident had happened to one of their own children.

I realised my father's beliefs about black people were wrong and it was possible for me to reason out problems like this.

In my first year of grammar school I was twelve. We had a camp in Pembrokeshire during the summer holiday. The party lived in an ex-military camp and worked all day in local farms. The nearest church was eleven miles away. I decided it was unreasonable to ask me to cycle that distance on my only day off. The camp was supervised by my history teacher whom I greatly admired. On that Sunday morning he asked me if I intended to go to church, I replied I did not.

'Yesterday evening', he said, 'after a hard day's work I heard you tell your friends you had cycled to Camarthen, a distance of fifty miles. Surely if you did that you could cycle to church.'

He was right so I did. I realised it is all too easy to make excuses for not doing necessary things.

At the age of eighteen I was waiting to go to medical school and my beloved grandma was dying of oesophageal cancer. She was dehydrated being unable to swallow fluids, even saliva, and was in considerable pain but never complained. Every evening all her children and myself gathered around her bed and prayed together. She looked fondly at us and I felt she was saying to herself, 'I have done a good job in bringing them up in the Faith.'

I thought when I come to die I hope I shall be able to say the same about my children.

The message:

We all have experiences which mould our faith. Never forget them.

On Miracles

The New Testament records the miracles performed by the Disciples. They were able to speak in the languages of their audience, walked out of locked prison cells and cured bodily ailments. What we would now accept as miracles probably do still happen but must be rare and we would seem to have no personal experience of them. Why is this so?

In the early days of the Church they were preaching a new religion founded by a carpenter's son from a remote part of the Roman Empire. Its doctrines were remarkable – forgiveness of sins, the Eucharist, and welcoming slaves as members. Any sophisticated Greek or Roman would have regarded these beliefs as madness. Miracles would have been a credible manifestation of the veracity of the Faith for such people. Subsequently, the visible examples of the good lives of Christians would remove the need for such spectacular demonstrations.

Having said this my own belief is that we are surrounded by miracles which we fail to recognise as God's interaction with our own lives.

When I was eighteen years old I spent a day in August caving in the Gower Peninsula. One of my friends had a folding boat with an outboard motor which could be carried on his car roof. We decided to go out into Oxwich Bay in the boat while still dressed in our caving outfits of boiler suits and boots. When we were about a mile offshore we went over a wartime shipwreck which ripped the bottom off the boat and we were pitched into the water. One of my friends was a strong swimmer and made it to a nearby buoy, which to our later embarrassment was meant to warn of the shipwreck below the surface. My other friend was unable to swim and clung to the boat wreckage. I could only dog-paddle so I circled the boat.

No one knew where we were and we were too far offshore for anyone to hear our cries for help. After about three hours we began to tire and became very cold and weak. The swell rose and the tide turned. It was now midnight and we would be swept out into the Bristol Channel and would clearly not survive until first light. I realised I was going to die and felt very sad because I would never be able to marry Rosemary whom I had met three months earlier.

Fortunately, a local man had decided on impulse, he might go fishing off Oxwich Point and heard us. He ran back to the beach where he kept a canoe. He summoned the life boat which would take an hour and a half to arrive and bravely set out in the canoe. He towed in my friend and myself, and the man who was relatively safe on the buoy was picked up by the lifeboat.

You may say, 'What a series of coincidences.' Rather more than this, we were exhausted, probably hypothermic; no one knew where we were and the tide was about to sweep us out to sea. A man happened to go out fishing, had excellent hearing, possessed a nearby canoe and was very brave. I had prayed for our rescue and feel that what happened was a miracle. Why God rescued me I do not know, nor what was his plan for me. Maybe to have someone to take a Communion Service at St Michael's Church sixty years later. I am sure many of you can recall experiences like this but our lack of faith means that we find it hard to recognise them.

The message:
Miracles still happen – thank God.

John Newton

(Author of the Song 'Amazing Grace')

Amazing grace! (how sweet the sound)
That sav'd a wretch like me!
I once was lost, but now am found,
Was blind, but now I see.

'Twas grace that taught my heart to fear,
And grace my fears reliev'd;
How precious did that grace appear
The hour I first believ'd!

Thro' many dangers, toils, and snares,
I have already come;
'Tis grace hath brought me safe thus far,
And grace will lead me home.

The Lord has promis'd good to me,
His word my hope secures;
He will my shield and portion be
As long as life endures.

Yes, when this flesh and heart shall fail,
And mortal life shall cease;
I shall possess, within the veil,
A life of joy and peace.

The earth shall soon dissolve like snow,
The sun forbear to shine;
But God, who call'd me here below,
Will be forever mine.

John Newton was born in 1725 and died in 1807. At an early age he joined the merchant navy but was captured by the press gang and forcibly enrolled in the Royal Navy. He hated it and deserted. He was soon recaptured and demoted from midshipman to ordinary seaman and flogged. He considered whether to commit suicide or instead to kill the captain. Fortunately, he did neither but his dislike of the captain seemed mutual. When the ship reached Madeira the captain exchanged him with a seaman from a slave ship. When that ship reached Africa the captain lent him as a slave to a local queen. She disliked Newton and when he was gravely ill with malaria she refused him food and drink. His weakness was so great that the other slaves pitied him and fed him.

When the captain returned the queen accused Newton of stealing from her; so when the captain's ship left to continue slaving, he manacled Newton to the open deck where he was exposed to the tropical sun and rain. The poor man declared that theft was the only sin he had not committed.

His father had not heard from his son so commissioned another captain about to sail for England to look for his son. Thus he was rescued and they sailed for Britain. During this time Newton came across a copy of the *Imitation of Christ* by the medieval author Thomas a Kempis. It made him think that if it was true that Christ had died for us then his life so far had been wasted.

When they were off the South Coast of Ireland they were struck by a severe gale. The hull was holed and they were with little hope of surviving. Newton remembered how his mother had taught him about religion and promised God that if his life was spared he would return to the practice of his faith. The cargo then shifted and fortunately plugged the hole in the hull and the ship limped into an Irish port. Newton did become a practising Christian but returned to work in the slave trade. He later admitted he was a ruthless businessman and brutally suppressed slave revolts in the ships he captained, lashing slaves and using thumb-screws.

In 1754 after a serious illness he gave up the sea and became an Anglican priest whose sermons were famous. He began to deeply regret his involvement in the slave trade and wrote, 'My confession is too late, it will always be a subject of humiliating reflection to me that I once was an active instrument in a business at which my heart now shudders.' He campaigned vigorously against the slave trade which was made illegal before his death in 1807.

The messages:

The sparing of Newton's life would have been because of a series of remarkable coincidences. We may feel that God directly intervened to rescue him as part of his plan for John.

The most dissolute are not beyond God's forgiveness.

A mother's teaching may be remembered in a time of crisis.

Saint Paul on Love

1 Corinthians – Chapter 13:

Love is always patient and kind; love is never jealous; love is not boastful or conceited, it is never rude and never seeks its own advantage, it does not take offence or store up grievances.

Love does not rejoice at wrongdoing, but finds its joy in the truth.

It is always ready to make allowances, to trust, to hope and to endure whatever comes.

Love never comes to an end. But if there are prophecies, they will be done away with; if tongues, they will fall silent; and if knowledge, it will be done away with.

For we know only imperfectly, and we prophesy imperfectly; but once perfection comes, all imperfect things will be done away with.

When I was a child, I used to talk like a child, and see things as a child does, and think like a child; but now that I have become an adult, I have finished with all childish ways.

Now we see only reflections in a mirror, mere riddles, but then we shall be seeing face to face. Now I can know only imperfectly; but then I shall know just as fully as I am myself known.

As it is, these remain: faith, hope and love, the three of them; and the greatest of them is love.

This is my favourite Epistle and I will book it for my funeral. You will remember Christ said, 'Do not worry about how to speak or what to say. The Spirit of your father will be speaking in you.' Paul was a humble tent-maker from a remote part of the Roman Empire and surely would not be capable of writing such lyrical poetry. I feel God must have put these words in his mind.

Paul does not define what he means by love. It may seem flippant to say that love covers a multitude of sins, but it does because our acts done out of love mitigate the sins we commit. That is a source of consolation because many of us will have children or grandchildren who seem to have abandoned their faith. When we pray for them we can say 'do not look at their weakness but rather at the love they have shown towards us.'

The love of which Paul speaks can be that of a woman and a man, a parent and a child, ourselves for everyone else of our faith and no faith. It includes atheists. The Jesuit Head of the Vatican Astronomy Observatory said he had no problems getting on with atheists because they had only one less God than him.

The other form of love expressed by the Epistle (and mirrored by ours) is the love of God for us and his willingness to forgive us out of love.

The message:

Love is at the centre of our Faith. If we have perfect love of our fellow humans and of God, then we will sin against no one.

On a Wedding Anniversary

We recently had a 55th wedding anniversary and it made me reflect on marriage and the family. I have been most fortunate in having a very happy marriage with four devoted children. Not everyone is so fortunate and when marriages fail we must not judge people but, as a community, support them.

People often ask me for my secrets of a happy marriage. First, Rosemary has not found out about me – yet. Second, instant obedience. Third, mutual respect which means I always have to respect her and remain mute.

One of the greatest responsibilities of marriage is raising children and transmitting the Faith to them. It is a mistake to swamp their minds with our religion and make them attend every service. Ultimately, they will resent this and rebel. Conversely, if we do not regularly attend mass and the sacraments it is unreasonable to expect them to do so.

We have all seen the situation often with the most devout parents where the children fall away from the Faith leaving the parent with a feeling that they have failed. There are consolations in this situation. Not all of the actions of these children are bad and they often do some very good things in their lives which God will recognise and reward. Again, children often return to the Faith, sometimes after traumatic events in their lives such as a divorce or even our death. Sometimes it happens for no apparent reason but the prayers of the parents. When our children have abandoned their beliefs and we appear before God maybe he will say, 'You had three children who abandoned their faith.' What do you say? I suggest, 'Lord I did my best.' He will have no answer and will welcome you in.

The message:
Do not despair if your children are not practising Catholics. Think of the good things they have done in their lives.

On Change

We Catholics are experts at sweeping under the carpet matters which are contentious or embarrassing. An example of the latter is the way in which, certainly in the past, the Church mishandled dealing with child sex abuse. It can lead to complacency and perhaps a sense of superiority for example feeling that, unlike the Anglicans, we do not tear ourselves apart by arguing about lady bishops or gay marriage.

A few weeks ago I talked about St Paul's embarrassing epistles when he advised wives to obey their husbands and slaves to serve their masters. I pointed out this was rather shady theology but wisdom accumulates with time and what is clear to us was not clear to Paul who held the conventional beliefs of his time.

If you look at some of the sea changes in our own beliefs over the last sixty years the change with time is obvious. When I was a child it was taught the there was no salvation outside the church. In India about one percent are Catholics. It is impossible to believe that a merciful God would condemn the other ninety-nine percent. Again we were taught that there were two kinds of sin: venial and mortal. For venial sins we had to spend an unknown period in Purgatory and mortal sins unless repented merited going straight to hell. I have not heard anyone preaching this for many years and the old belief in Limbo for unbaptised children has vanished without a trace. Indulgences are still around but young people seem very sceptical.

A year ago one of my children went on holiday to Rome and returned telling me of luxurious hotels and much wining and dining.

'Not exactly a pilgrimage', I said sarcastically.

'Ah dad but I did go to a church which gained me a plenary indulgence.' Some may well say Luther got it right!

We live in rapidly changing times and must be ready to discuss all sorts of new issues but need to do so in a spirit of tolerance and charity towards those who hold different opinions to us.

The message:
The church is changing rapidly after a long period of inertia. We should welcome this and not be frightened by it.

The Disciples as Failures

I find it very encouraging that the disciples were such failures. This seems a strange thing to say and I will explain my statement.

Look at Peter. He failed Christ when he fell asleep in the garden and then at the court of the High Priest he denied that he even knew him. At the crucifixion, like all the Apostles save John, he ran away. Yet he was a man who had lived with Jesus for three years, had witnessed all his miracles and acknowledged that Jesus was the son of God. He was entrusted with leadership of the church. How disgraceful that with such a background he would subsequently behave so shamefully.

St Thomas refused to believe that Christ would rise again but after this account he vanishes from the Bible. In the fifteenth century the Portuguese discovered Kerala in South India. They found a church which, although it had a different liturgy, was evidently Catholic. They were members of the Syriac Rite founded by 'doubting Thomas' according to local belief in AD 50.

Before becoming a Christian St Paul had approved the stoning to death of St Stephen and had held the cloaks of the executioners. These three people are loved and rightly respected members of our early church. They had done some terrible things yet God forgave them and trusted them to spread his word.

The message:

God forgave these men who had badly sinned. I am sure none of us would deny God or murder Christians. How much more readily will God be to forgive our lesser sins.

On Judging People

A week ago I had a telephone call from a Columban priest call Aodh O'Halpin. He told me a story I would like to share with you.

I have known Aodh for more than 30 years. He spent several decades of his life working with very poor communities in the Philippines.

When our daughter got her degree, for a year she had two jobs. One was as a paid part-time cleaner and the other was as an unpaid volunteer with the Philippine Support Group. At that time 30 years ago the Marcos dictatorship controlled the Philippines. In those days, foreign families coming to stay in Britain were allowed to bring their servants with them on their employer's passports. Most of the employees were from the Philippines although there were also many from Africa and Sri Lanka. If the servant wanted to leave their employer they were without a passport and were immediately sent home. The result was that many were exploited by their employers. They were not paid, worked cruelly long hours and were often physically and sexually attacked. The Philippine Support Group helped these people financially and helped with their efforts to be paid, sometimes bringing criminal charges against the employers.

The next little account is nothing to do with the homily but I know you all like a good story. At the end of working for a year Bridget sent in her tax return. She declared her earnings for the year were £750. The tax inspector called her for an interview and suggested she had not declared her whole income. He pointed out that no-one could live on an annual income of £750. Bridget insisted she was telling the truth.

'All right, do you smoke?'

'No.'

'Do you drink?'

'No.'

'What do you eat?'

'I buy 56lb bags of industrial rice and 56lb bags of beans which I make into curry.'

'You don't seem to have an address. Where do you sleep?'

'I stay free with various girlfriends from college.' The inspector sighed and said,

'This is such an unlikely story that it must be true. Just go away.'

At the end of the year Bridget decided that she would go away to the Philippines for a year. This was a dangerous move because anyone sympathising with the poor was labelled by the Marcos Regime as a communist and likely to be jailed, tortured or even killed. The regime was rather frightened of the church which was very influential in that part of the world. Aodh O'Halpin got the head of the Columban order to give Bridget a letter addressed to all Columban priests saying she was to be given any help wherever she was. This was a useful insurance policy.

Three years ago Aodh baptised Rosemary and received her into the church, a process which had taken me 55 years. I am greatly indebted to him.

The story Aodh told me in a phone call a week ago was that in Nigeria the Columbans work closely with an order of nuns. Three of these nuns were in a car in a quiet country road near Kano. You will remember that this area of Nigeria is where the fanatical Boko Haram movement is very active. They kill Christians and those Muslims who do not agree with their intolerant beliefs. The nuns' car suddenly broke down. They were stranded without mobile phones and no RAC! A few moments later a car drew up behind them and out jumped three young men. Their prayer hats and robes immediately identified them as Muslims and the nuns were terrified when they approached the car. They enquired what the problem was and lifted the bonnet of the car. They joined two broken wires together and the car restarted. The nuns apologised that they were so suspicious and explained their fears of Boko Haram. One of the men said, 'Tomorrow is Friday and I will go to the Mosque. If Allah asks me why did I pass three Christian women in distress and did not help them, what would I say?'

The messages:

Never classify people. In the first world war we did not fight German people but the Hun. In the Falklands it was the Argies. The Daily Mail labels Roma as thieves and pickpockets and benefits claimants are always scroungers.

The vast majority of Muslims are good, kind people and share most of our values.

On St Peter's Toe

Ordinary everyday events in our lives can sometimes make us stop and think. In St Michael's church we have embarked on stripping and replacing the plaster of the church interior. Unavoidably, this process emits large amounts of dust. A few weeks ago we were going to have a funeral service for an old friend of the church. Out of respect for him and perhaps, out of a wish to show off our beautiful church to a new large audience attending the funeral service, it was decided that the church would be cleaned on the morning of the funeral.

A group of volunteers turned up. Rosemary believes that my skills around the house are such that I should only be trusted with simple tasks such as carrying heavy objects over level ground and even then only under close supervision. My reputation had preceded me so I was given a feather duster and instructed to dust the statues.

The last statue was at the rear of the church facing the door and was a life size metal statue of a seated St Peter. Starting at the top I came to his big toe, tickled it with the duster and noted the part had worn away leaving bare polished metal. Curiously, the left big toe was the only part of the statue not made of metal and had been replaced by wood. What had happened was that as people left or entered the church they had kissed the Saint's toe out of devotion to him. The church is almost 130 years old so the part had eventually worn off. The left toe was nearest the central aisle and the door and had become so worn that it had to be replaced.

This made me realise how much the people of the parish loved their church. The beautiful stained glass windows were constructed around 1904. If they were done today it would probably cost two to three million pounds yet this done by one of the poorest communities in Newport.

The love of the church continues. In the past nine years the church has collected approximately eighty thousand pounds for restoration of the fabric and this has proceeded apace. No doubt we are all fed up with the dust and dirt engendered by the long re-plastering activity but we have a duty to hand on a well maintained church to future generations as our ancestors did for us.

The message:
Well done St Michael's.

The Love of God

I was brought up by loving Catholic parents, was an altar boy, attended mass every week and went to Catholic primary school.

At the age of twelve I lost the plot, God meant nothing to me although I continued to attend mass on Sunday because not do so would have grievously hurt my parents. During this time of life my driving forces were entirely selfish and I must have been a rather unloveable child, I was certainly unhappy.

During my fourteenth year I began to feel the presence of God and by the time I was fifteen I was certainly back firmly in the fold. This does not mean I became a saint but at least turned into a standard Catholic sinner.

We believe that whatever sins we commit, from genocide down, if we ask for God's forgiveness then we get it. In my instance I did not ask for forgiveness but God so loved unloveable me that he came and sought me out. Whenever I pray I always start by saying 'thank you Lord for saving me'.

The message:
God so loves us that he not only forgives our sins when we ask him but his grace recalls us to the faith in spite of our weakness.

On Heaven

When we feel depressed or ill or are bereaved it is comforting to think of heaven when we will have no worries and will meet again with all the people we have loved or have gone before us.

However, such thoughts can bring a sense of anxiety. It is like sitting an examination and not knowing the pass mark. We look at the lives of the saints and think of how many good things they did compared to our own poor efforts and how many bad things we have done during our own flawed lives. When we think like this there are two comforting lines of thought.

The first is that we tend to underestimate the good things we do. How many good people have diligently looked after sick parents or have tried hard to bring children up in the Faith or persisted with their own during times of stress or emotional difficulties. Again we forget the small acts of kindness we regularly do such as visiting the sick or consoling the bereaved. How many of you in this church regularly donate to CAFOD for the relief of poverty? Christ said that as much as you do these things unto the least of my brethren you do them to me. We may forget these good deeds but God does not.

The second line of thought is that our sins may be so great that God will not forgive them. An American lawyer was committed to helping on death row. When asked how he could possibly want to help such wicked people he commented that no man's life should be judged by his worst action. I am sure that God feels like that and no matter how bad our sins they are forgiven if we ask for it.

The message:

All our sins are forgiven if we ask for it and no one is beyond God's mercy.

At Eastertide

Christ showed himself to many people after His resurrection. Mary the mother of James spoke to Jesus whom she initially assumed was a gardener until she recognised Him. The disciples did not believe the accounts of the woman who has seen him. This probably reflected the times because in Jewish courts women were regarded as unreliable witnesses (it is not for me, a mere male, to question the wisdom of the Sanhedrin!) A second initially unrecognised appearance was on the road to Emmaus.

Jesus also appeared to the Apostles at a mountain near Galilee, on two occasions at Lake Tiberius and on two further occasions in a locked upper room where they were hiding for fear of the Jews.

At Christ's death the Apostles must have been in despair. They had left their families and work and had followed Him for three years only for it all to end with his shameful death on the cross.

We are told they greeted His appearance in the upper room with joy. Everything would have fallen into place. As He foretold he had risen from the dead after coming to save the world. The Apostles were inspired to go out and preach the good news and in the case of Peter he was so convinced that he was prepared to suffer martyrdom.

The message:

At Easter we can join with the Apostles in celebrating the resurrection of Christ. Sometimes they failed to recognise Him. Perhaps He appears to us and we do not recognise Him when He appears in the guise of people who need our help or sympathy and we fail to provide it.

On Learning from Mistakes

I will tell you two stories. At first hearing they may not seem relevant to religion but their relevance will become apparent.

When I was a medical student the first two and a half years were spent without seeing patients but learning about subjects such as anatomy and physiology. Over the next three years students spent three months in a variety of medical specialties such as obstetrics and anaesthetics.

My first specialty assigned was in medicine and I was allocated to the firm of Dr (later Dame) Francis Gardner who was the rudest, cleverest woman one could possible meet. I was apprehensive because she had a reputation for being fierce especially towards incompetent students. She instructed me to take a history from a new patient, to examine him and then to present the case to her. The G.P letter stated that the man had a heart murmur and a previous history of tuberculosis which was now cured.

An hour later the great woman strode into the cubicle accompanied by her entourage and five students in my group who had come to enjoy the fun. I thought I presented the case rather well and concluded that the murmur was due to a narrowed aortic valve but did not require treatment because the heart was not enlarged and there was no breathlessness. It would be reasonable to review him in two or three years time.

'Is that the only important finding?' asked Dr Gardner. I stated that was so. 'Walk across the room' she told the man, whereon he fell over and was clearly unable to walk. I panicked,

'He isn't drunk', I bleated.

'That will be a great consolation to Mr Jones', Dr Gardner replied. She then asked me how his tuberculosis had been treated and from my thorough history I told her with streptomycin. She then asked me what were the side effects of that drug and realisation dawned. It destroys the part of the inner ear that deals with balance explaining why he cannot walk. 'Idiot!' she said and walked out.

I was rather depressed but over the next few days realised that patients do not spend their lives in a doctor's examination couch and that I would subsequently watch the ways in which patients walked. It often proved very helpful.

Forward to 1970. I appointed a Chinese Malay doctor to a junior post and he was very clever and enthusiastic. One night my team was on duty and Dr Foo telephoned me in the middle of the night to say he was worried about a woman in her forties without a previous history of lung disease who had been admitted with a chest infection. She was very agitated and to calm her down Foo had given her a small dose of intravenous Valium. Within ten minutes she became unconscious. I went into the hospital and she was desperately ill with very shallow breathing and dangerously low levels of blood oxygen. She had always smoked fifty cigarettes daily and her bronchitis was clearly chronic and more severe. I pointed out to Foo that such patients were exquisitely sensitive to respiratory depressant drugs such as Valium which caused them to stop breathing. I told him that we will put her in a ventilator and within 48 hours she will be back to what passes as normal for her and that is what happened.

To our mutual humiliation she subsequently gave us each a bottle of whiskey for saving her life. Foo was devastated and asked me how he could have made such a dreadful mistake. He needed cheering up and I told him he should have seen some of the mistakes I had made during my career but the lesson was not to make them again.

The message:
We all make mistakes in our lives. The lesson is not to keep making them.

On Forgiveness

God must have a great deal of forgiving to do. What prompted this thought is recently reading about the history of the Ravensbruck concentration camp in Germany during the Second World War.

This institution was initially constructed to house female prisoners but later included both sexes. The most appalling atrocities and tortures were practised here. Initially, priority was in killing Jews, the sick and Russian prisoners, but it soon became indiscriminate for every class of prisoner. The methods used were brutal; the sick in batches of up to eighty would be locked in a room without heating, food or water. When the doors were opened a week later they would all be dead. Others were hanged or beaten to death and towards the end of the war gas chambers were built with the target of killing 2000 a month.

The guards were usually young men, though occasionally women, who were likely to have been raised as Catholics or Protestants but what they were doing was clearly incompatible with their beliefs. A variety of excuses were subsequently made; everyone else did it, if I did not do it someone else would so ultimately I made no difference, if I did not do it then I would have been executed or sent to almost certain death on the Russian front. None of these excuses are acceptable, no guard was executed for disobeying orders and only one was sent to the Russian front and this for stealing property which should have been sent to the Gestapo.

One Senior officer wrote frequent letters home to his wife and they were often about what he had for dinner the previous night. He grumbled about overwork because he had to complete 150 forms a day. He did not mention these were details of inmates to be sent to Auschwitz for extermination. There were dozens of such concentration camps scattered over Nazi controlled Europe.

A rather superficial explanation of their behaviour is to say there is something peculiar about the German nation and our brave lads would never do anything like that. Don't believe it, I know a few people who would have volunteered to be concentration camp guards. A few days ago I read an account of a British soldier who had terrible pangs of remorse for the rest of his life after the war. He was angry at the death of some of his platoon and threw a grenade into a pillbox where German soldiers were surrendering carrying a white flag. Like the camp guards during war, combatants regard the enemy as lesser human beings and dehumanise them by clarifying them as Jews, Argies or Ragheads – it makes them easier to mistreat.

After the war, surviving camp guards returned to their homes. They must have been ashamed to share their experiences with family and friends. Many, with time, must have re-joined the practice of their Faith and realised the enormity of what they had done. How could they ask for the mercy of God when they themselves had shown none?

Remember no one, no matter how grave their sin, if they truly repent, is beyond the mercy of God. What a remarkable thing that He can still love and forgive people who have done such appalling things.

The message:
No one is beyond the mercy of God.

On Morality Without Religion

Most of my friends and neighbours do not practice any religion. They may have a faith but it is not apparent. They are not bad people and do not do obviously evil things. The guide to their behaviour seems to depend on the general principle that they should not be unpleasant to other people. That is unless they are gypsies seeking to set up a site near their homes, or Muslims against whom they sometimes advocate wars whilst condemning the irresponsibility of surgical strike bombings – after all they have principles. They may disapprove of euthanasia or abortion but when these problems enter the lives of their families these beliefs may suddenly change.

We do not know how God will judge their lives but we can be sure it will be with mercy and understanding of the difficult dilemmas they may have faced.

Such people may say that it is easy for you Catholics because you have a rule book which provides rigid guidance but for us the rules may sometimes be very difficult to keep. Remember that surely God will expect more from us than people without belief who do not even know that what they do is wrong. Christ told us we should be a leaven – an example to the Gentiles so that our influence exceeds our numbers.

When I was a child the nuns taught me that every night we should consider and repent the sins we had committed that day. Equally important, in order to cheer us up we should think of the good things we have done. These do not have to be heroic but are usually small things like talking to someone who is lonely.

The message:

God expects more of us than those without belief. Not only do we need to avoid sin but positively to do that which is good.

On Being Eighty

I recently celebrated my eightieth birthday. It certainly concentrates the mind to be this age and perhaps the first thought is that one is on overtime and the question is what dreadful and possibly painful illness will soon arrive. There is little point in dwelling on this as there is nothing we can do about it.

An alternative, more positive approach is to consider the benefits of being old. For many our worries are less. We spend less, have paid off our mortgages and thus have fewer financial worries, our children have grown up and while we still worry about them there is not the same day to day anxiety as when they lived at home.

There are certainly spiritual consolations. We will have sorted out what we believe and how we practice our faith. Our big mistakes are behind us and repented. If we have stuck to our faith so far then we are likely to finish the course.

In our hearts we want to live indefinitely, but in our minds we know this to be impossible. When we die we leave behind all the worries of daily existence and are promised eternal happiness. We do not know what form this will take but God has not let us down so far and will not do so in the future.

The message:

As we grow old do not dwell on the unpleasant things which may happen. Rejoice in the present and trust God.

On the Week After
Trinity Sunday

My memory of sermons on Trinity Sunday is that the priest starts by saying that the Blessed Trinity is a mystery which we cannot understand. They then try to explain it and, understandably, do not do very well. It has been said that more heresy is preached on Trinity Sunday than on any other Sunday of the year. One must have sympathy for these poor priests and I certainly would not wish to proceed in their footsteps but suggest that we look at the Trinity in a different way.

Enemies of religion say the idea of three persons in one is not feasible and beyond rational thought and this confirms the Christian religion is nonsense. I would contest this by describing what is known about the electron. According to quantum theory, the electron is simultaneously both a wave and a particle and can be in two places at once. This is, surely, a more difficult concept that the Trinity but it would be foolish to conclude that all science, therefore, is nonsense. We would be greedy to think that with our limited intelligence we would expect to know everything about God.

In imagining the Father I recall my own father. My parents had four children. I was one of three boisterous boys given to constant unarmed warfare. For those without boys in the family this is normal. In wartime there was strict food rationing and no mechanical aids such as washing machines or refrigerators. The life of my mother must have been extremely stressful. After a particularly naughty period my mother snapped and said that when dad came home she would tell him to smack us. This was accepted practice at the time and is not to be judged by current standards of child care. We waited in trepidation and heard my father being given his instructions. We heard him say, 'I cannot do it Eileen my hand is too heavy.' Like my father, God the Father would forgive me and tell me not to do it again.

Christ is the easiest to imagine, well described in the Gospels and a man like me in all things save sin. When he walked his feet ached and he felt tired. Like me he sometimes felt depressed or lonely and was occasionally angry, but unlike me his anger was always justified.

For the Spirit there are two obvious ways of seeing Him (or Her!). The first is when we are bereaved or suffering He stands besides us. The other is at times of great happiness. A few weeks ago all my children and grandchildren came to visit us on my 80th birthday and came to a mass to celebrate is. Our children's choir sang beautifully. Being Welsh and emotional I had a quiet cry and felt God beside me.

The message:
Next Trinity Sunday think of these aspects of God. I guarantee them free from heresy.

On the Year of Mercy

Pope Francis announced this year would be a Year of Mercy and made two low key announcements which really reflect a large change in the way the Church thinks.

The first is that women who have an abortion are automatically excommunicated and are only released from this after confession to a bishop or a specifically authorised priest. The new rule is that they can go to any priest. Remember that the decision to have an abortion may have resulted from extreme circumstances or pressure from other people and may have been followed by terrible guilt. Can you imagine some poor woman plucking up the courage to go to confession at her local church only to be told she must start again and go to the bishop or some distant, authorised priest?

The second announcement was about the process of annulment of marriage. Annulment still means that for some good reason the marriage should not have happened. Examples might be that a woman married only to obtain security for her child or that she was mentally incapable of giving her consent at the time.

Previously the process required a two stage tribunal at different places and was an extremely slow and expensive procedure beyond the financial cost for many people. The Pope said there would now be a free way with a single local tribunal.

In the Old Testament we are often told that God is merciful but he was depicted as being very hard on sinners. In past years in the matters of abortion and marriage annulment the Church has certainly had a rather Old Testament approach. The recent announcements by Pope Francis are important because they are ways of bringing God's help and forgiveness to sinners.

The message:

The Pope has brought practical application to the Year of Mercy.

On Loneliness

Loneliness is an increasing problem in our world. The characteristic victim is an older person often a widow or widower who has outlived the family and we all know such people. My mother was a widow for ten years and died at the age of 92. She was desperately lonely and further cut off by severe deafness. She lived in Swansea and I would make the 100 mile round trip once a week after a day's work. Whenever I got up to go she would either embark on a long story to keep me there or accuse me of always being in a hurry. I usually started work at half past seven in the morning and after visiting her would get home at ten in the evening for dinner, so the accusation was unfair but understandable.

Loneliness is an increasing problem among young people. They often have to move from home to a new job or to attend university and this can make the feel very alone. I certainly found this on going to London.

God understands loneliness because he experienced it Himself. He left his family in his teaching mission and was often met with rejection of his message and vilified. At his crucifixion he must have felt desperately lonely when he was deserted by his disciples and most of his followers.

The message:

If we feel lonely God understands and will always be at our side. St Paul had a vision of Christian communities where the people support each other. We have a duty to support the lonely in our own communities.

On Bad News

When we watch the news it easy to get despondent about the way God runs the world. We look at the awful things happening in Syria, Palestine or the Congo and despair. You will remember the Israelites rebuked God for abandoning them in the wilderness when they had been promised a future land of milk and honey.

It is worth remembering that most of the awful happenings in our world are the result of the work of man (I would admit rarely of woman!). We should remember that what seem to be unending hopeless conflicts do change. In Germany the Nazi regime fell, the Northern Ireland conflict ended in peace and various dictators have been overthrown. God's time is not our own. A recent news item reminded of this.

The Lubyanka jail in Moscow was the torture centre for Stalin's secret police. He would tell them that two and a half percent of the population were traitors and subversives and the police needed to find them. Large numbers of people would be arrested and then tortured until they admitted their crimes. They would then be either executed or deported to a lingering death in Siberia. If the police found less than two and a half percent of the population guilty then they too would be interrogated, found guilty and sentenced. The news item was that this dreadful jail was to be converted to an Orthodox church.

The messages:

What appear to be hopeless situations usually resolve with time and God does not desert us.

Disasters are usually the result of failings of people.

On the Depiction of God in the Old and New Testament

In the Old Testament there are two consistent themes in describing the actions of God. One is that He was often punishing his people by exiling them or visiting them with plagues, droughts and famines. The other is of His mercy when following their repentance of their sins He forgives them and removes these burdens.

The depiction of God in the New Testament is not of a punishing God but one who is always ready to forgive and full of mercy. Such dual visions of God seem impossible. They demand an explanation.

The accounts of the events in the Old Testament and the actions of the Prophets were often written hundreds of years after the events they describe and are thus unlikely to be factually accurate accounts. It would be likely that the Jews sought reasons for the bad things that had happened to them. Disasters such as drought, famine and disease are always with us and happen in an irregular and unpredictable fashion. The Jews would have regarded them as logical punishments for their transgressions.

When the Lord looks at our modern world he must sometimes become discouraged when he sees wars and countries in which many are starving whilst others live in luxury. He must get consolation from the lives of the Saints but they are all dead.

He must get consolation when he sees parishes like our own with a strong bond of firm believers who lead the sort of lives prescribed by the Apostles. They are not recognised as Saints but their good lives are seen by God. I suspect for many in this congregation when they die and are at the gates of heaven the Lord will say, 'You are a girl from St Michael's in Pill, come on in.'

The message:

The depiction of a harsh, punishing God often described in the Old Testament is likely to be a misinterpretation of Him.

On the Seventieth Anniversary of Hiroshima and Nagasaki

A Catholic priest, Father George Zabelka, was the chaplain to the American Air Force Group who dropped the nuclear bombs in Hiroshima and Nagasaki and subsequently wrote an apology.

In 1975 he suddenly realised that he had been brainwashed and told the attack was necessary. He had blessed the men who had dropped the bomb.

'I was wrong', he said, 'Christ would not have been the instrument to unleash such horrors on his people. Excuses and self-justifying explanations are without merit. Last year in Japan I asked for forgiveness from the survivors of the bombs. I prayed for forgiveness for myself, my country and my Church. Each of us becomes responsible for the crime of war by cooperating in its preparation and execution. This includes the military and those paying for the weapons.'

'I watched the bomber taking off for Nagasaki piloted by an Irish Catholic. The aiming point for the bomb was the Catholic Cathedral – the centre of Japanese Catholicism. I knew schools, churches and religious orders would be annihilated and I said nothing. The central step in the process of renunciation is the admission of guilt.'

Father Zabelka died in 1992.

The message:

The use of nuclear bombs is immoral and incompatible with our faith.

On Parables

In the Gospel readings on Sunday we often listen to parables but they sometimes come with problems. They may use fifty words to say something which could be accomplished by ten. Occasionally they seem patronising as though we are incapable of understanding the basic tenets of our Faith. Some are difficult to understand such as the vineyard labourers who all got the same pay in spite of working for very different periods of time.

Why did Christ use parables? It seems this was the normal method of teaching at that time. Over time, methods of teaching and communication do change. An example is that in Eastern Europe before the war, among Yiddish speaking Jews, if asked how they were they would never reply that they were in excellent health and prosperous. Such a happy situation was a gift from God and he could withdraw it if someone boasted of it. A typical response would be 'my worst enemy should feel like this.'

Sometimes parables contain an important hidden subtext. The parable of the Good Samaritan tells us we must look after the weak and the sick. The subtext is the Levite priest who passed by on the other side of the road. We are not told why he did this, perhaps he was in a hurry or knowing that if he touched a bloodstained man he would become unclean and would have to take a ritual bath. The Samaritan belonged to a group of people despised by the Jews and the parable tells us that we cannot judge by appearances.

Again Christ wants to tell us that repentant sinners are forgiven. This is beautifully done in the parable of the Prodigal Son. He had spent his father's money and lead an immoral life but the father welcomed him home – a clear analogy with the love of God. The subtext is the behaviour of the brother who resents the easy forgiveness of the father and fails to understand it. When we see people who have committed terrible sins such as genocide or offences against children we can fail to see how such people can be forgiven if truly repentant.

The message:

The parables make the truths of our Faith evident with practical examples. It is worth looking for subtler messages which they often contained.

On a Controversial Pope

It is customary that when Popes travel abroad they tend to speak in vague generalised terms and it often needs a skilled Vaticanologist to determine what they are really trying to say. Pope Francis recently went to America and totally overturned this tradition and attacked some of the beliefs held by many Americans.

America is the second largest arms exporter in the world. Its arms trade is an important source of economic activity and national income. Francis said it was immoral.

Another popular idea is that all Mexican and South American immigrants should be sent home. Francis said, 'I do not think they have considered who would then clean their swimming pools, dig their gardens and look after their children.' It's also hypocritical because they themselves are the descendants of largely economic migrants and sometimes of asylum seekers. Francis told them that they should be welcomed.

Many Americans firmly believe in the death penalty and Francis told them it should be abolished. I feel it is wrong for a variety of reasons. It is cruel and often involves the deliberate infliction of pain. The Romans did this with crucifixion and Edward I in England introduced hanging, drawing and quartering for rebels and traitors. The condemned were tied to a hurdle and dragged, often over cobbles, while being stoned by the mob. They were then hung, but not to death and then cut down and disembowelled and finally quartered. The Americans still, in some states, use the electric chair with the occasional person being fried to death. In addition, there must be the mental agony of waiting for death often after a period of up to ten years through multiple fruitless appeals.

Innocent people are often executed and the availability of DNA technology has shown they could not possibly have committed the crime for which they were killed.

Capital punishment removes time for repentance. None of us have the same personality as we did twenty or thirty years earlier and many, given time, would come to repent their sins. Finally, we did not ask to be born and life is a gift from God. It is for God to take back and not us.

The message:
How good to have a Pope who tells it like it is.

Dealing with Illness and Bereavement of Friends

One of the things we do badly is dealing with friends who have been told they have a fatal illness or who have suffered the death of a close family member. When we meet these friends we often feel we do not know how to help them or what to say. In my professional life I have dealt with about 3000 patients who died of lung cancer and tens of thousands dying of other conditions yet I still feel incompetent in friends facing death.

A useful way to start is by asking an open question such as asking how they or their family are coping. This gives them an opportunity to talk which seems to help the problem and all we have to do is listen. If outside the regular Sunday mass there is one for the deceased or dying and we attend that mass, the family will feel comforted. If all else fails, just give them a hug.

There are two good examples of comforting people in my mind. You will remember that a local Saint, David Lewis, who was a Jesuit priest was sentenced in Usk in 1679 to be hung, drawn and quartered. From the scaffold he forgave his persecutors and judges. He was extremely popular and the county sheriff refused to attend the execution while the largely Protestant spectators insisted, that contrary to the usual practice, he should be hanged until dead before being disembowelled. He had always been very friendly with the local Anglican clergyman who held his hand while he was being strangled and refused to bury him under the church door where, as a sign of contempt, people would trample over his body.

The other example is when Pope Francis visited the Greek island of Lesbos where 30,000 asylum seekers were abandoned with little hope of finding a safe place of refuge. The Pope made it clear that himself and the Church were standing by them. He said all Catholics had an obligation to help refugees. Many Catholic European countries had refused their help and the Pope's words must have shamed them. He was accompanied by the Head of the Greek Orthodox Church. The two churches have barely spoken since the Great schism of 1054 and this was a significant meeting. He returned to Rome with twelve refugees, all Muslims, to be cared for by a Catholic charity and said the only qualification for them was that they were God's children. What a man, what a leader.

The message:

Do not worry about meeting people in this situation. Do your best and God will help you.

On Persecution of the Church in Syria

We went to Syria for a holiday about 25 years ago. Foreign tourists were clearly unusual but we were made to feel very welcome. At that time the country was ruled by the father of the current President Assad. It was a very repressive regime with a network of informers everywhere. Before going we were advised that these people would try to entrap us into saying something indiscreet. If someone asked you your opinion of President Assad, then the safe thing was to say that he was a very clever man.

Our guide told us that in a previous tour a very brash American bemoaned there was no freedom in Syria. He expounded that in America he could stand up in the central square in Washington and shout out that President Ford was a **** and no one would attack him. The guide replied that if he stood up in Martyr's square in Damascus and said that President Ford was a **** not only would no one attack him but everyone would applaud.

There were two striking features about religion in Syria. The first was the amount of religious history. We visited a plateau where there was still standing a pillar in which St Simeon Stylites had passed most of his life.

This was surrounded by about thirty visibly destroyed churches ruined under the persecution of the Roman Emperor Diocletian. On a lintel of one of these was an inscription which stated it had been built by Simon the Deacon in the year 282. At a functioning church nearby we heard the Our Father being said in Aramaic, the language of Christ. In this church the stone altar had a rim around the edge. This was because the rim was to contain the blood of animal sacrifices when it was a pagan temple. The Council of Chalcedon banned the reuse of such altars for Christian worship so the church must have predated this. We also visited the town of Palmyra which had been buried by sand and excavated about 100 years ago. This was on the old Silk road from China and was the Easternmost reach of the Roman Empire where there was a well preserved temple dedicated to Baal and dating from 200BC.

The other remarkable feature of Syria was the number of religions and how well they got on. There were all varieties of Islam, Shia, Sufi and Alawites. Amongst the Christians were Syrians, Greek and Russian Orthodox and Catholics. One woman said they were originally Orthodox but one Saturday night a much loved grandmother was evidently dying. Her son went out to get an Orthodox priest but, being a Saturday and raining heavily, the priest said he would not come until the next day (when granny might be dead). On the way home he met a Franciscan priest who agreed to give her the last rites. The next day grandmother miraculously recovered and the family had been staunch Catholics since.

All this has been destroyed. The church with old pagan altar was wrecked and the Christians fled when

ISIS captured the village. The monuments at Palmyra were destroyed. The various religious bodies are not at peace and the Christian population have largely left Syria.

The message:

Religious persecution is still with us and we pray that peace may come to Syria.

On the Rise in Infant Baptisms

Ten years ago baptisms in St Michael's church were uncommon. In the last two years in all six churches in our combined All Saint's Parish group there has been a steep rise in their numbers. Surely a cause for rejoicing, yet listening to parishioners there are signs of discontent over three aspects.

The first is that they make the Sunday mass overlong and people say they prefer the older system where baptisms were held separately when those attending were almost entirely just family and friends. But baptism is about welcoming someone into our community and we do not do this if we do not attend the ceremony.

This was beautifully demonstrated at a recent baptism when, at the end of mass and a baptism, our deacon held the baby up and presented him to the congregation to spontaneous applause.

Another complaint is that the relatives often have no idea about how to behave in church or what baptism is all about. They often dress as for a disco, chew gum throughout and answer their telephones. The latter is especially irritating and happened to me when giving a homily. I advised the recipient of the call not to worry as it was only the babysitter asking where they kept their fire extinguisher.

Probably around ninety-five percent of Newport inhabitants do not know what happens at a Catholic mass. What a marvellous opportunity to show them. Make them feel welcome and at the sign of peace look as though you mean it. At the end of the service talk to the parents. You may say that you never know what to say. It is easy. Just say, 'what a lovely baby' and offer your congratulations – this is always well received.

The final reservation is that parishioners say that we shall never see the parents or the child again. These parishioners are bestowing upon themselves the gift of prophesy. Personally I can never accurately predict what will happen tomorrow let alone in thirty years time.

The message:

Let us rejoice in the increased numbers of baptisms. We would have good cause to be unhappy if the number was falling.

Advent and the Understanding of Christ and Who He Was

It is challenging to think of God being born as a helpless infant. Clearly because He was like us in all things then he would only have had the understanding of any new born child. His only worries would be whether he was comfortable, hungry or needed a cuddle from his mother. As he grew up Mary would have surely taught him how to pray and he would have been a pious Jewish little boy who spent a lot of time in the Temple and reading the scriptures. We know this because when He was left behind in Jerusalem by his parents they found He had astonished the doctors of religion in the Temple with his knowledge for one so young.

The next account in his life is the miracle of Cana when he turned water into wine. By this time He must have realised that He was the Son of God.

It must have been terrifying when He gained knowledge of the manner of His forthcoming death especially as He must have seen people being crucified. It was always a public spectacle designed to frighten people into keeping the Roman laws. He must have been often despondent when, knowing he was going to make this sacrifice that people refused to accept his teaching and even his disciples deserted him during His passion.

The message:

It must have slowly dawned on Christ as to who He was. Imagine our emotions if we knew we would be crucified.

On Lent

We have a much easier Lent than our medieval ancestors. During Lent they did not eat meat or dairy produce and ate only one meal a day. The Coptic Church still sticks to these rules with no smoking and Lent lasts for fifty days.

If you ask Catholics what they are doing for Lent most would reply, 'nothing', and some would tell you what they are giving up. We seem to have gone astray in the manner in which we keep Lent but a good general intention is to seek to be better Christians at its end than at its beginning. It is worth looking at our lives to see how we can achieve this.

There are three strands to Lent, prayer, good deeds and self-denial. We may feel that we are not very good at formal prayer but do not be discouraged. Every day for five or ten minutes you can read the Gospels or the New Testament. Personally I find the Old Testament rather boring and full of smiting and punishment. Once a week decide to go to a service and I would particularly recommend the Stations of the Cross. For thirty-five years we have attended Friday evening Stations with our local Church in Wales parish.

Good deeds are always available. There are simple acts of kindness which do not have to be heroic – perhaps speaking to someone you know to be lonely or unpopular. Forgive an enemy. You may say that you have none, then forgive yourself. We may dwell on past sins forgetting that God has told us they are already forgiven if we have asked Him to do so.

Finally, we have our old standard of penance. The foundation of heaven will not be shaken if we give up chocolate. An important reminder is not to behave like the Pharisees and announce what we are doing. They looked miserable to tell others they were fasting. As Christ said, 'I tell you solemnly they have had their reward.'

The message:

If, so far, you have failed during Lent, try again. If you have not yet started do so today.

During Holy Week

The portrayal of Christ in the Gospels is one of a fearless character. He strode into the temple and overturned the tables of the moneylenders. As a child, after having been left behind by his parents in Jerusalem, he disputed with the Doctors of theology. Again he told the Jews that he was the Son of God, which they interpreted as blasphemous and intended to execute him for these words. When he preached around Israel He must have often met crowds who were hostile to His teaching. We are told that Christ was like us in all things save sin, but we would never have the courage to do these sorts of things save for a few saintly examples.

The side of his life which we can readily understand is the story of the Agony in the Garden when He was vulnerable and frightened. Matthew tells us a sadness came over him and a great distress. He said, 'my soul is sorrowful to the point of death, keep awake with me. Nevertheless, let it be as you not I would have it.' Needless to say the Apostles did not watch with Him but fell asleep three times and deserted Him in His hour of need. Mark gives a similar description and Luke tells us that in his anguish the sweat fell to the ground likes drops of blood. Here then is evidence that Christ experienced despair, foreboding fear and was truly like us.

The message:

When things go wrong and we are frightened God understand our anxieties because he too has experienced the same emotions.

On Christ Raising
People from the Dead

The most striking of Jesus' miracles were when on three occasions he raised people from the dead. When He entered the city of Nain a body was being carried out of the city gate. It was of the only son of a widow and Jesus raised him to life.

A man called Janus went on his knees to implore Christ to save the life of his twelve year old daughter. Shortly after the news arrived that the girl had died. Christ said to Janus, 'only have faith and she will be saved.' He went to the house where the family and friends were mourning and announced that the child was not dead but asleep. The idea seemed so ridiculous that in the midst of their mourning the crowd laughed at the idea. Jesus then restored her to life.

On the death of Lazarus, Jesus knew his sisters Mary and Martha and the Gospel tells us that he loved Lazarus. St John records that succinct, moving sentence: 'Jesus wept.' Lazarus had been dead for four days but when Jesus called him from the tomb the live Lazarus emerged.

Why did Christ perform these three remarkable miracles? There seem two likely reasons. The first is compassion. The poor widow of Nain was likely to be left in severe poverty and loneliness. There were two major sects of Judaism, The Sadducees who did not believe in an afterlife and the Pharisees who did. The Sadducees believed that if you led a good life, and this included strict adherence to the dietary and Sabbatical rules, then God rewarded you with health and prosperity. If the widow was a Sadducee – and we do not know this – her neighbours would conclude that her miserable life as a widow without children was a reward for a sinful life and she deserved little sympathy. For the death of Janus' daughter who among us would not have been moved by the death of a child.

The second reason for these miracles was that Christ was proclaiming revolution and He was claiming to be the Son of God to an unbelieving, sceptical people. Here we have a poor carpenter's son from a remote part of the Roman Empire, not even an aristocrat or even a Levite. Judaism has an intricate network of rules of behaviour. On the Sabbath, Orthodox Jews still cannot put on a light switch or push a child's buggy to the synagogue because this is regarded as work which is forbidden on the Sabbath – you will remember that the Jews rebuked the Disciples because they picked an ear of corn on the Sabbath. Jesus spotted their hypocrisy and asked which of them would not rescue his ox if it fell into a pit on a Saturday. Unlike the Jews he entered the house of tax collectors and ate with them. He even claimed to forgive sins which to the Jews was blasphemy.

His actions in raising the dead demonstrated that He was God. When He raised the widow's son we are told the people said that God has visited his people.

The message:

These miracles show the compassion Christ has for us in our bereavements.

On Walking Through
a Local Graveyard

Every morning to pick up my newspaper I walk through our very large cemetery which opened in about 1880, and this walk certainly makes me think.

In one section is a large collection of graves of Rosminian priests many of whom had been known to me. One was an old priest called Father Huish who had become increasingly confused but insisted he was still fit to drive his car. Eventually the inevitable happened and he drove into a bollard. The police recognised that he was unfit to drive and gave him a choice. He could go to court and would have inevitably have been found guilty, banned from driving and, no doubt, featured in the local newspaper. The alternative was to hand in his driving license voluntarily when no legal charge would be made. Under pressure from his superiors he reluctantly accepted the second course. His car was given to a younger priest but this rankled with the old man and at two o'clock one morning he filled a bucket with icy water and threw it over the bed of the younger priest.

Burials from the Victorian era are concentrated in one part of the cemetery. The graves are often topped by statues four or five metres high which must have cost the modern equivalent of £10-20,000. The inscriptions often parade their achievements such as a title Captain, Councillor or Alderman. The neighbours might be impressed with these manifestations but it is unlikely that the Lord is too impressed.

At the other end of the site is the area reserved for Catholics who would regard themselves as ordinary unimportant people often well known to me. They are not unimportant to God. When John Hurley died God would have said, 'You are the man who looked after the fabric of St Michael's Church all your life and never sent a bill.' To Jimmy Williams, 'you served on the altar for nearly eighty years.' To Alison Goodwin who died tragically in a riding accident aged seventeen, 'You took handicapped children horse riding and brought happiness to their lives.'

The message:
God judges differently to the way the world does.

On the Murders at a French Satirical Magazine

Everyone was horrified when two groups of fanatical Muslims killed thirteen people at the office of a French satirical magazine and four others at a Jewish delicatessen in Paris.

The murders at the magazine were characterised by the media as a quarrel between freedom of expression and a group of men who had developed a fanatical misunderstanding of Muslim beliefs. I can agree with this description of the murderers but the magazine had previously been criticised for anti-Semitism and was confessedly against Islam and Christianity. Its beliefs were in the traditional line of hatred of religion which dates from the French Revolution in 1789. To mock someone's deeply held beliefs is at best bad mannered and discourteous, and at worst dangerous. The authors must have known they were at risk of rousing dangerous hatred by their actions which had also resulted in the murder of an innocent Muslim policeman.

An American judge with the delightful name of Learned Hand once said that freedom of speech does not allow you to shout 'fire' in a crowded theatre. The murders in the Jewish delicatessen were equally abhorrent. To confirm that the beliefs of the murderers are not those of other Muslims it is of note that a Muslim employee at the shop saved five customers by hiding them in a fridge. This employee certainly risked his own life because the assailants would be likely to have killed him if they knew what he had done.

The message:

We live in a cosmopolitan world with people of different religions and none. Where opinions differ we must never mock the beliefs of others but treat them with respect and tolerance.

On Faith

We are told that God loves us all but there are certain groups to whom He seems particularly devoted.

In the Sermon on the Mount they are recalled; the poor in spirit, those that mourn, the meek, those who hunger and thirst after justice, the pure in heart, the merciful and those reviled and persecuted for the sake of God.

There is another group whom He particularly loves and that is those with Faith. I will not recall all the Gospel references to them because the list is very long. When the men lowered the paralytic through the roof to meet Jesus He told them the man was cured because of their Faith. The woman who touched the hem of His robe was told that your Faith has saved you and He made the same statement when he cured Bartimaeus the blind beggar.

Matthew also gives examples of the miracles performed on people who were not Jews. When the centurion asked for his servant to be cured and said that Jesus could do this without even coming to his house Christ said that not even in Israel had He found greater Faith. The Canaanite woman who was cured was also a Gentile. The love of God was not confined to the Jews.

Luke tells us that during the Last Supper Jesus prayed that Peter's Faith would not fail. John does not use the word Faith but on more than one hundred occasions uses the word 'believe'. Theologians could probably argue indefinitely between the meaning of the words Faith and believe but we could agree that they overlap. For example, when addressing Doubting Thomas Christ said, 'blessed are those who have not seen and yet believe.'

The messages:

Our Faith in God makes us closer to him.

Faith is easy when everything in our lives goes well but may be tested when they go badly wrong. If we maintain our Faith God stays with us.

On Death

It has been said that the only inevitable thing in life are death and taxes. You will be relieved to hear that this evening I do not intend to speak about taxes.

We rarely talk about death because it seems to make us uncomfortable. A few weeks ago I read a remarkable article on the subject in The Tablet by Jonathan Riley Smith, a professor of Ecclesiastical History at Cambridge University. He was told that he had a short time to live and has died since the text was published. I have always been involved in caring for the dying and during my career have attended about three thousand patients with lung cancer and tens of thousands with the other diseases which afflict us. His advice elegantly crystallises thoughts which I have felt in a rather vague fashion and I will give a short summary.

- Some would like a sudden death without warning and sparing suffering. This is likely to leave extensive and burdensome tidying up work and a long warning gives time to set one's affairs in order.
- A good death brings peace to the family.
- Enjoy the life left to you, make the most of it and be grateful.

- Life is a gift from God and we do not have the right to end it.
- My faith was strengthened by the terminal illness. Faith and illness became intertwined and became part of each other.
- Remember your life has been a preparation for this.
- Do not become consumed by unnecessary guilt although it is good to make peace with anyone you have offended.
- Treat death as a celebration.
- Plan your funeral.
- Leave your relatives with good memories of your death. Your fortitude will ensure they remember you with pride and affection.
- Avoid quack remedies from well-meaning friends. They will only offer forlorn hope.

The message:
There are too many to list.

Epilogue

Lay-led communion services will surely become a necessity because of the shortage of priests. For several years I have done these weekly in my local parish and have learnt many lessons:

- Speak slowly and make sure the microphone is working well.
- Three or four minutes is enough
- Talk about experiences in your own life which have strengthened or challenged your faith.
- Tell them what good people they are not that they are sinners.
- After the service I always feel depressed because I have already said everything I could think of and do not want to become repetitive. I then go for a week and by the next week words appear.
- Unless you are a teacher, public speaking is frightening. If you lose your thread (what actors call the dries) the congregation are supportive and willing you on.
- Tell them what you are going to say, say it, then tell them what you said by giving them a message. A sermon with no message is pointless.
- Only tell funny jokes.

Lightning Source UK Ltd.
Milton Keynes UK
UKOW03f0624190417

299386UK00001B/5/P